Defining
MOMENTS
OVERCOMING CHALLENGES

Franklin Delano
ROOSEVELT

Nothing to Fear!

by Deborah Kent

CONSULTANT
Joseph A. Pika
University of Delaware

BEARPORT
PUBLISHING

New York, New York

Credits
Cover and title page, Courtesy FDR Library; 4, ©Hulton-Deutsch Collection/CORBIS;
5, Courtesy FDR Library; 6, ©CORBIS; 7, Courtesy FDR Library; 8, ©Bettmann/
CORBIS; 9, ©CORBIS; 10–11 (both), Courtesy FDR Library; 12–14 (all 3 photos),
©Bettmann/CORBIS; 15, Courtesy FDR Library; 16–21 (all 6 photos), ©Bettmann/
CORBIS; 22, ©CORBIS; 23, Courtesy FDR Library; 24, ©Associated Press, AP; 25,
Courtesy of FDR Library; 26–27 (both), Courtesy of National Park Service.

Publisher: Kenn Goin
Project Editor: Lisa Wiseman
Creative Director: Spencer Brinker
Original Design: Fabia Wargin

Library of Congress Cataloging-in-Publication Data
Kent, Deborah.
  Franklin Delano Roosevelt : nothing to fear! / by Deborah Kent ; consultant, Joseph
Pika.
      p. cm. — (Defining moments. Overcoming challenges)
  Includes bibliographical references and index.
  ISBN-13: 978-1-59716-272-2 (library binding)
  ISBN-10: 1-59716-272-8 (library binding)
  ISBN-13: 978-1-59716-300-2 (pbk.)
  ISBN-10: 1-59716-300-7 (pbk.)
  1. Roosevelt, Franklin D. (Franklin Delano), 1882–1945—Juvenile literature. 2.
Presidents—United States—Biography—Juvenile literature. I. Title. II. Series.

  E807.K46 2007
  973.917'092—dc22

                        2006005313

For more information, write to Bearport Publishing Company, Inc., 101 Fifth Avenue,
Suite 6R, New York, New York 10003. Printed in the United States of America.

10 9 8 7 6 5 4 3 2 1

Table of Contents

"The Only Thing We Have to Fear" 4

A Lonely Child 6

Winning the Votes 8

Polio 10

Warm Springs 12

A Big Return 14

From Despair to Hope 16

A New Deal for Hard Times 18

Bombs over Pearl Harbor 20

Going to War 22

The End of the Road 24

Memorial for a President 26

Just the Facts 28

Timeline 28

Glossary 30

Bibliography 31

Read More 31

Learn More Online 31

Index 32

About the Author 32

"The Only Thing We Have to Fear"

On March 4, 1933, Franklin Delano Roosevelt stood on the steps of the U.S. **Capitol** in Washington, D.C. He was being sworn in as the 32nd president of the United States.

Franklin was sworn into office by Chief Justice Charles Evan Hughes. Franklin's son, James, and former President Herbert Hoover stood behind him.

During his **inauguration** speech, Franklin spoke in a strong voice. "The only thing we have to fear is fear itself," he said. Franklin knew these words well. He had worked hard to conquer fear in his own life. Twelve years before, **polio** had destroyed the muscles in his legs. He needed help standing and walking. Now, in spite of everything, Franklin was about to lead the country during its hardest times.

Franklin is the only president who has ever been elected to four terms in office. Today, by law, the president can serve only two terms.

When Franklin was elected president, thousands of people were out of work, homeless, and hungry. During his speech, Franklin reassured Americans that he would make things better.

A Lonely Child

Although Franklin would grow up to lead millions of people, his early years were very lonely. He was an only child and spent most of his time with adults. Instead of attending school, he studied at home with teachers.

Franklin at age ten

At boarding school, Franklin (top row, center) became the manager of the school's baseball team.

In 1896, at age 14, Franklin left his family's home in Hyde Park, New York, to go to boarding school. Later he went to Harvard and then studied law at Columbia University. Franklin liked **politics** more than anything else. He looked up to his cousin, Theodore Roosevelt, who had spent years in government. He had been president of the United States from 1901–1909.

In 1905, Franklin married Eleanor Roosevelt. She was a great support to Franklin during his life.

Winning the Votes

In 1910, Franklin ran for state **senator** in New York. With no experience, few people thought he would win. Franklin led a strong **campaign**, however, and easily won the election. As senator, he came up with **bills** that protected land and helped farmers and poor people.

Franklin, age 28, addresses supporters during his campaign for senator

Three years later, President Woodrow Wilson called Franklin to Washington, D.C. The president asked him to be the assistant secretary of the Navy. Franklin was delighted that his new job included two things he loved: ships and the sea. Franklin tried to make the Navy strong. He also helped this military group get ready for World War I (1914–1918).

Franklin's cousin, Theodore, had been the assistant secretary of the Navy years before Franklin. Theodore went on to become the youngest person ever to serve as U.S. president.

As assistant secretary of the Navy, Franklin (far left) spent time on naval ships all over the world.

Polio

In the summer of 1921, at age 39, Franklin and his family took a vacation. They stayed on the island of Campobello, off the coast of Maine. One night Franklin suddenly fell ill with a high fever. By the next day, he couldn't walk. Both of his legs were **paralyzed**.

This is the last known photo taken of Franklin walking without help.

*Franklin's doctor (right) created
a tough exercise program for
him to follow.*

Before there was a **vaccine** for polio, it killed or crippled thousands of people each year, mostly children.

Eleanor brought in a doctor who told Franklin that he had polio. He would never be able to walk again. However, Franklin wouldn't believe it. He wanted to lead the life he had before getting polio. He decided to do everything he could to get back on his feet and return to politics.

Warm Springs

Franklin went from one doctor to another, trying to find someone to help him. He underwent many painful treatments. None of them were very helpful. Then he heard about the mineral water at Warm Springs, Georgia. Many people said that the spring water had the power to make people healthy again.

Even though Franklin couldn't walk, he was able to drive. His car had hand controls instead of foot pedals.

Franklin enjoying a swim

Franklin bathed and swam at Warm Springs. Sadly, the water didn't cure him. However, being there helped Franklin in another way. He was able to relax. He swam every day and enjoyed the warm sunshine.

Franklin wanted other people who had polio to be able to visit Warm Springs. He helped turn it into a treatment center that became famous around the world.

13

A Big Return

Seven years after becoming ill with polio, Franklin returned to politics. He thought voters would only choose a person who looked strong. For this reason, he hid his **disability**. He let his warm smile and confident words earn the trust of the American people. In 1928, he was elected governor of New York.

Franklin casting his vote during the election for governor

During the Great Depression, people often had to wait in line for food.

The following year, the **Great Depression** hit. Banks closed, factories shut down, and millions of people lost their jobs. Hungry people walked the streets looking for work. As governor of New York, Franklin tried to change things. For example, he created new jobs and helped the poor get housing and food.

When Franklin stood before a crowd, someone was always by his side. He balanced himself on the other person's arm. It looked, however, like he was standing on his own.

From Despair to Hope

Meanwhile, President Herbert Hoover was having a harder time helping the rest of the country. Franklin decided to present his ideas and run for president. In his campaign, he promised to make the country strong again. People listened. On Election Day in 1932, Franklin became the new president.

Franklin, his family, and supporters celebrating his win

Since it was hard for Franklin to travel, Eleanor became his legs. She went around the country for him and visited poor people. She told Franklin about everything she found while on her trips.

In May 1935, Eleanor visited coal mine workers in Ohio.

Few Amercians knew that Franklin couldn't walk. They didn't know that he used a wheelchair in the White House. People wanted to believe that their president was strong. In fact, Franklin was even stronger than they knew. He lived with great pain, but he didn't complain. He wanted to give the American people hope and confidence.

A New Deal for Hard Times

In the 1930s, most Americans were afraid that the country would never get through the Great Depression. Farmers and workers struggled to make money. Millions of people didn't have jobs. So Franklin developed the **New Deal** to create jobs and help poor people. He put thousands of people to work building schools, hospitals, and playgrounds.

Franklin's New Deal program helped farmers get paid fairly for their crops.

Franklin used the radio to reach Americans through a series of shows called Fireside Chats.

The New Deal was not liked by everyone. Some poor people thought Franklin wasn't doing enough to help them. Some rich people said his programs hurt banks and businesses. However, most Americans felt he gave them hope for a better future. Franklin was elected to a second term in 1936.

Bombs over Pearl Harbor

During the 1930s, other countries were also going through a depression. Some of them were easily taken over by **dictators**, such as the German leader Adolph Hitler. During 1939, he invaded much of Europe. When some countries fought back, World War II broke out. At first, the United States stayed out of the war.

In 1940, Italy joined forces with Germany. These Italian troops are getting ready to attack.

Then on the morning of December 7, 1941, Franklin got some terrible news. Japanese planes had bombed the U.S. Navy at Pearl Harbor, Hawaii. Many of the nation's ships had been destroyed. Franklin knew the attack meant that the United States would have to enter the war.

In the late 1930s, the United States struggled with Japan. During Franklin's third term, the Japanese decided to support Germany and Italy in World War II. This move led to the attack on Pearl Harbor.

The battleship USS Arizona sank into Pearl Harbor after being bombed by Japanese planes. During the attack, 21 ships were damaged and about 2,400 people were killed.

Going to War

The United States was not ready to fight a war. Its Army was small and had few planes or weapons. Franklin had to find a way to quickly make the equipment and supplies needed to win the war.

In 1944, Franklin was elected to his fourth term as president. Harry S. Truman was his vice president.

Franklin visits with American troops.

Franklin asked Americans for help. He promised that the country could win the war if everyone worked together. He pushed factories to make weapons, uniforms, planes, and warships. By the early 1940s, almost everyone in the United States was helping to fight the war in some way.

During World War II, women went to work in the factories.

The End of the Road

By 1945, the United States and its **allies** were winning. Sadly, Franklin never saw the return of peace. His heart was failing. He grew tired and thin. Sometimes he could hardly sit up in a chair.

The Yalta Conference, held in 1945, brought together British Prime Minister Winston Churchill (left), Franklin (center), and Soviet Premier Josef Stalin (right). The conference was held to discuss ways to stop the war.

In April 1945, Franklin went to Warm Springs for a much needed rest. He died suddenly a few weeks later. The nation went into **mourning** for its leader. Franklin was buried in the garden of his childhood home in Hyde Park, New York.

A special funeral train carried Franklin's body from Warm Springs, Georgia, to Washington, D.C. People lined the tracks to watch the train pass by.

Memorial for a President

Franklin Delano Roosevelt was a fearless leader. During times of little hope, he found ways to make life better for the American people. In 1997, a **memorial** opened in Washington, D.C., to honor him. The outside rooms are filled with statues and pictures. The photos show Franklin during his years as president.

In this area of the Franklin Delano Roosevelt Memorial, tall pillars represent the New Deal.

When the memorial first opened it didn't show Franklin using his wheelchair. People with disabilities protested. In 2001, the statue of Franklin in a wheelchair was added.

The memorial includes one statue of Franklin seated in a wheelchair. The world could finally see that although Franklin had a disability, he never let it stand in his way. Franklin is remembered as a great president. He is also remembered as a man of courage and strength.

Just the Facts

■ As a child, Franklin Roosevelt was fascinated with birds. He collected nests, eggs, and even stuffed birds.

■ At Harvard, Franklin was not a great student, but he made many friends. After his lonely childhood he loved being around people his own age.

Timeline

Here are some important events in the life of Franklin Delano Roosevelt.

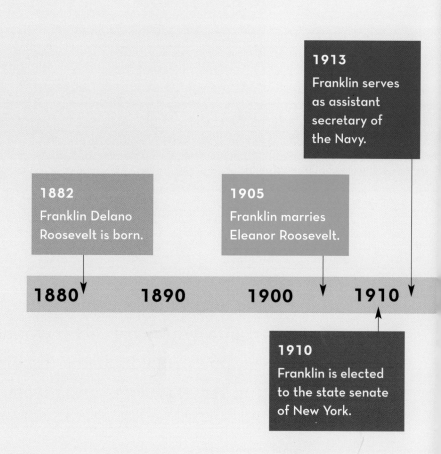

1913
Franklin serves as assistant secretary of the Navy.

1882
Franklin Delano Roosevelt is born.

1905
Franklin marries Eleanor Roosevelt.

1880   **1890**   **1900**   **1910**

1910
Franklin is elected to the state senate of New York.

■ Franklin and Eleanor Roosevelt had six children. One son died when he was a baby.

■ Throughout his life Franklin loved sailing. After he had polio, sailing and swimming were activities he continued to enjoy.

■ The press helped Franklin hide his disability. Photographers never took pictures when his aides were carrying him up stairs.

■ In 1935, Franklin signed the Social Security Act. This program put aside money for millions of retired or disabled Americans. Many people believe that Social Security is one of Franklin's greatest achievements.

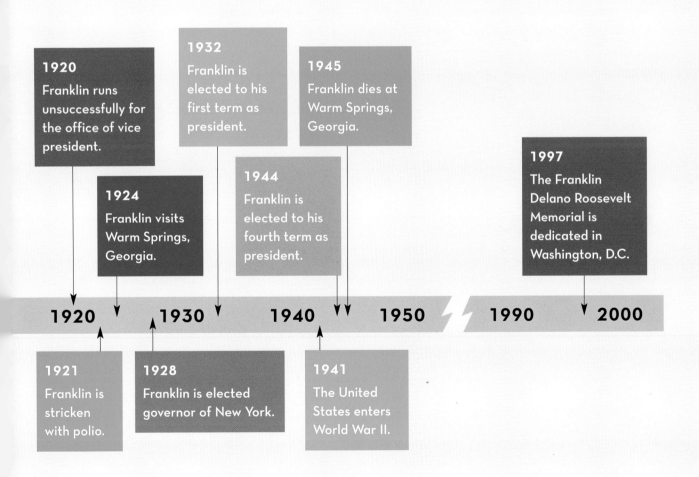

1920
Franklin runs unsuccessfully for the office of vice president.

1924
Franklin visits Warm Springs, Georgia.

1932
Franklin is elected to his first term as president.

1945
Franklin dies at Warm Springs, Georgia.

1944
Franklin is elected to his fourth term as president.

1997
The Franklin Delano Roosevelt Memorial is dedicated in Washington, D.C.

1921
Franklin is stricken with polio.

1928
Franklin is elected governor of New York.

1941
The United States enters World War II.

1920 1930 1940 1950 1990 2000

Glossary

allies (AL-eyez) friends or supporters

bills (BILZ) written plans for new laws

campaign (kam-PAYN) an attempt to win a political office

capitol (KAP-uh-tuhl) the building that serves as the center of government

dictators (DIK-tay-turz) people who have complete control over a country and usually run it unfairly

disability (diss-uh-BILL-uh-tee) a condition that makes it hard for a person to do everyday things such as walking, seeing, hearing, learning, or caring for him or herself

Great Depression (GRAYT di-PRESH-uhn) the period of time from 1929 through the 1930s when many people in the United States lost their money, jobs, businesses, and farms

inauguration (in-aw-gyuh-RAY-shuhn) a ceremony where public officials are sworn into office

memorial (muh-MOR-ee-uhl) something that is built to honor a person or an event

mourning (MORN-ing) to feel very sad for someone who has died

New Deal (NOO DEEL) President Franklin Roosevelt's program to help the United States recover from the Great Depression

paralyzed (PA-ruh-lized) unable to move

polio (POH-lee-oh) a contagious disease that attacks the brain and the spinal cord; it can cause paralysis

politics (POL-ih-tiks) everything to do with running for and holding public office

senator (SEN-uh-tuhr) a member of the lawmaking body of government

vaccine (vak-SEEN) medicine that protects people against diseases

Bibliography

Black, Conrad. *Franklin Delano Roosevelt: Champion of Freedom.* New York: PublicAffairs (2003).

Howard, Thomas C., and William D. Peterson, eds. *Franklin D. Roosevelt and the Formation of the Modern World.* New York: M. E. Sharpe (2003).

Jenkins, Roy, Arthur Meier Schlesinger, and Richard E. Neustadt. *Franklin Delano Roosevelt.* New York: Times Books (2003).

www.pbs.org/wgbh/amex/presidents

Read More

Emerson, Judy, and Gail Saunders-Smith. *Franklin Delano Roosevelt.* Mankato, MN: Pebble Books (2003).

Feinberg, Barbara Silberdick. *Franklin D. Roosevelt: America's 32nd President.* Danbury, CT: Children's Press (2005).

Haugen, Brenda. *Franklin Delano Roosevelt: The New Deal President.* Mankato, MN: Compass Point Books (2006).

Phillips, Anne. *The Franklin Delano Roosevelt Memorial.* Danbury, CT: Children's Press (2000).

Learn More Online

Visit these Web sites to learn more about Franklin Delano Roosevelt:

www.fdrlibrary.marist.edu/fdrbio.html
www.ipl.org/div/potus/fdroosevelt.html
www.nps.gov/fdrm/home.htm

Index

Army 22

campaign 8, 16
Campobello Island 10
Capitol 4
Columbia University 7

disability 14, 27, 29

Fireside Chats 19
Franklin Delano Roosevelt
    Memorial 26–27, 29

Germany 20–21
governor 14–15, 29
Great Depression 15, 18

Harvard 7, 28
Hitler, Adolph 20

Hoover, President Herbert
    4, 16
Hyde Park, New York 7,
    25

inauguration 4–5
Italy 20–21

Japan 21

Navy 9, 21, 28
New Deal 18–19, 26
New York 7, 8, 14–15,
    28–29

Pearl Harbor 20–21
polio 5, 10–11, 13, 14, 29

Roosevelt, Eleanor 7, 11,
    17, 28–29
Roosevelt, Theodore 7, 9

senator 8, 28
Social Security Act 29

Truman, Vice President
    Harry S. 22

vaccine 11

Warm Springs, Georgia
    12–13, 25, 29
Washington, D.C. 4, 9,
    25, 26, 29
wheelchair 17, 27
Wilson, President
    Woodrow 9
World War I 9
World War II 20–21,
    22–23, 24, 29

Yalta Conference 24

About the Author

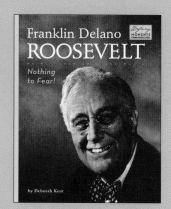

DEBORAH KENT grew up in Little Falls, New Jersey. She has written nearly two dozen young-adult novels and numerous nonfiction books for children. She lives in Chicago with her husband, children's author R. Conrad Stein, and their daughter, Janna.